BRITAIN'S PRIME MINISTERS
Power and Parliament

Number 10 Downing Street: much photographed, much visited. Many famous figures from the history of the past 300 years have passed through this front door.

It is a short walk from 10 Downing Street to the Houses of Parliament. The much-photographed front door has been the gateway to power for more than 50 men and one woman: Britain's Prime Ministers. Ever since Sir Robert Walpole in the early 1700s, the Prime Minister has been the fountainhead of power in government. The Prime Minister chairs the Cabinet, sets the political agenda, appoints and fires ministers, and advises the sovereign when Parliament should be dissolved and a general election held. With Britain in Europe, and devolution in Northern Ireland, Scotland and Wales (which have their own first ministers), the office of Prime Minister still remains the ultimate goal for party leaders.

Politics and the United Kingdom have changed much in almost three centuries of the premiership. Each Prime Minister has faced different challenges; some have towered above their contemporaries, figures of national stature by virtue of talent, impact on national affairs, or sheer longevity in office. Their names headline our history.

This guide to Britain's Prime Ministers outlines the history of the great office of state, explains how the role of the Prime Minister has changed, and relates the lives and times of some famous holders of the office, interwoven with Britain's national story. Every Prime Minister has played a part in that story, and left a footprint in the corridors of power.

First First Minister

Today, the Prime Minister's power far exceeds that of the monarch, and has grown considerably during the evolution of the office. Not officially head of state, the Prime Minister frequently represents Britain on the international stage, and through its well-oiled media machine Downing Street spins and nudges national news.

The concept of a royal counsellor is an ancient one. Powerful churchmen and nobles stood at a king's side, or even ruled for him with the powers of princes. In the 1500s, Wolsey, Cromwell, Burghley and Cecil served their Tudor monarchs Henry VIII and Elizabeth I; but although Parliament was slowly gaining more power the monarch remained supreme until the Civil War of the 1640s, when Charles I resisted Parliament and lost his head. So perished the notion of the monarch's 'divine right' to reign and rule. This revolution gave Parliament the upper hand. After the Restoration of Charles II as king in 1660, an inner group of ministers, the 'cabal' (from which the Cabinet evolved), effectively ran the government. The Glorious Revolution of 1688–89, removing James II and bringing to the throne William III and Mary, shifted the balance of power again, in favour of Parliament.

The accession of King George I in 1714 led to the emergence of a 'first minister'. The term had been applied to Cardinal Richelieu in France in 1624, but the English disliked the notion of a Prime Minister, a position 'not enough understood to be liked' according to 18th-century

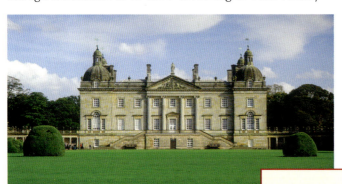

ABOVE: Houghton Hall in Norfolk, the country home of Sir Robert Walpole and his heirs. Britain's first Prime Minister and his two wives are buried in the church here.

ABOVE RIGHT: Walpole (1676–1745) lectures his Cabinet; illustration by Joseph Goupy (c.1680–1768). Walpole's ability to manage his ministers, and public money, made him the supreme politician of his age.

Whigs and Tories

A Whig was a 'horse thief', a Tory a 'papist outlaw'; the precise origins of these pejorative Gaelic and Scottish terms are debated. George I believed the Whigs were his defence against Jacobites (supporters of the ousted James II and his kin). Many Tories were plain conservative country gentry, but Toryism was discredited after the failed Jacobite uprisings of 1715 and 1745. For most of the 18th century the notion of 'party' did not exist, as power shifted between noble families and wealthy commoners jostling for royal patronage.

historian Gilbert Burnett. George I, the new Hanoverian king, German-speaking and ill at ease in the tangled Court politics of England, believed he owed his throne to the politicians known loosely as Whigs, and distrusted their opponents, the Tories, as pro-Jacobite and pro-Catholic. Unable to follow discussions in English, the king stopped attending Cabinet meetings. From 1721, the leading Whig, Robert Walpole (1676–1745), took the chair and became in effect Britain's first Prime Minister.

Knighted in 1725, Walpole stayed in the Commons to control the purse-strings of government, until elevated to the Lords as Earl of Orford in 1742. He was the Member of Parliament for King's Lynn (with one brief break) for 40 years. Walpole owed his supremacy to divisions among his rivals (Tory leader Bolingbroke fled to France), skilful use of royal patronage, and his friendship with Caroline, Princess of Wales, whose husband became George II in 1727 – as reliant on Walpole as George I. First Lord of the Treasury and Chancellor of the Exchequer, Walpole was the supreme political conjuror – even caricatured as such, complete with wand. Frequently accused of malpractices, he survived the speculative mania of the South Sea Bubble (1720–21), until a mismanaged war with Spain in the end brought him down; he retired, immensely rich, to enjoy his art collection and a unique position in prime-ministerial history.

LEFT: King George I in martial mode, painted by Sir Godfrey Kneller (1646–1723). During the German-born king's reign (1714–27), Walpole effectively led the country.

The Kit-Cat Club

Political gossip and deal-making went on in salons and London coffee-houses. The Kit-Cat Club, named after Christopher Cat's eating-house, was a favourite with Whigs in the early 1700s. Walpole and the Duke of Newcastle were members, enjoying the mutton pies for which the club was famed.

1740s–1830: Evolution and Revolution

1740s–1780s: Reigns of George II and George III

Walpole's power made him unpopular. Secure in royal patronage, he sacked any minister who challenged his policy. MP Samuel Sandys complained that a Prime Minister who sought to interfere with other departments was 'inconsistent with the Constitution of this country and destructive of liberty'. The moral climate was censorious, with accusations of corruption in high places and suggestions that the Court of George II was a thieves' den.

Walpole's immediate successor, the Earl of Wilmington (Prime Minister 1742–43) raised tax on brandy, but then died in office. Henry Pelham (1743–54), who introduced the term 'budget' while Chancellor of the Exchequer, oversaw the defeat of the Jacobites (1745) and Britain's switch to the Gregorian calendar (1752) when people rioted, demanding 'give us back our 11 days'. Pelham's brother, the Duke of Newcastle (1754–56), led Britain into the Seven Years' War with France. The victorious war, fought largely at sea and in North America and India, was directed by William Pitt, 'the Elder'. The Duke of Devonshire (1756–57), Newcastle again (1757–62), and the Earl of Bute (1762–63) led Britain post-war. An enthusiastic botanist and amateur actor, Bute was the first Scot and the first Tory to be Prime Minister.

ABOVE RIGHT: William Pitt, 1st Earl of Chatham – Pitt the Elder (1708–78). Pitt started his parliamentary career as a fierce opponent of Walpole, and made his reputation as a war leader in the 1750s. A compelling speaker, he was the first Prime Minister to dominate the Commons by oratory.

RIGHT: *Chairing the Member* by William Hogarth (1697–1764). Hogarth made four prints satirizing the Oxfordshire election campaign of 1754; in this final picture, the victorious MP is chaired by his supporters; rowdiness, brawling, beer and bribes were all seen as part of 18th-century electioneering.

LEFT: The British surrender at Saratoga, 1777. This 19th-century illustration shows General Burgoyne offering his sword to the American commander, General Gates.

In 1760, George III came to the throne. Pitt's brother-in-law, the Whig George Grenville (1763–65), the king thought tedious: 'when he has wearied me for two hours, he looks at his watch, to see if he may not tire me for an hour more.' Strapped for cash, Grenville raised taxes on the American colonies. His 1765 Stamp Act, hated by the colonists, was repealed by his liberal-minded successor, the Marquess of Rockingham (1765–66). When Rockingham's government collapsed in July 1766, the 'great commoner' Pitt (now Earl of Chatham) became Prime Minister, as Lord Privy Seal rather than First Lord of the Treasury. He was a waning power; though leading lights the Duke of Grafton, the Earl of Shelburne, Lord North and Charles Townshend joined his administration, it lasted only two years. Chatham died in 1778, collapsing in the Lords while making a speech.

Grafton struggled for reconciliation with the American colonists, without success. North (1770–82) was heavy-handed; his policy led to the Revolution of 1776, humiliating defeat and the loss of the colonies. Shelburne (1782–83) and the Duke of Portland (1783) negotiated peace with the new United States, and its allies France and Spain. Every Prime Minister had to cope with the increasing stubbornness of George III, whose bouts of illness were treated as lunacy. Britain's infant industrial revolution bawled largely unnoticed; the manufacturing classes were unrepresented in a Parliament dominated by county gentry and MPs voted in by tiny electorates in 'rotten boroughs' – constituencies with a handful of electors, where bribery and corruption at elections were rife.

10 Downing Street

Downing Street takes its name from Sir George Downing (1623–84). Born in America, this 'perfidious rogue' (Samuel Pepys' verdict) switched from Cromwellian to Royalist, and made his fortune from property development in London. One of his cheap terraced houses (Number 5) acquired a much grander addition in 1677 and had several owners before in 1730 it was offered by George II to Sir Robert Walpole. Walpole accepted the house as an official residence for the First Lord of the Treasury – and so it has remained, being renumbered Number 10 in 1779.

Law and order

In the 18th century Britain had no regular police, but harsh penal laws. Riots were common: against turnpike roads in the 1730s, food riots in the 1750s, 'Wilkes and Liberty' marches in the 1760s, and violent anti-Catholic disturbances (the Gordon Riots) in 1780. Hangings were public spectacles, from which a lordly title offered no protection; Lord Ferrers was hanged in 1760 for killing his servant, and his body handed over for anatomical dissection.

ABOVE: Prime Minister Lord North (1732–92) was blamed for inept policy and military failures, leading to the loss of the American colonies. This satirical drawing shows North asleep, a befuddled driver of the coach of state.

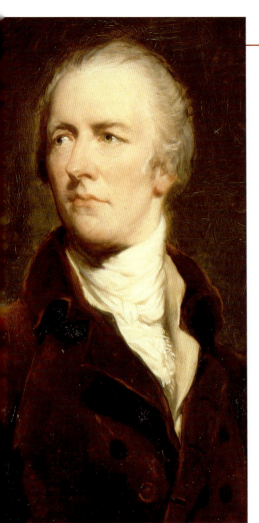

ABOVE: Pitt the Younger (1759–1806). 'I have never known his equal,' wrote William Wilberforce of Pitt's integrity and love of country.

RIGHT: This Gillray cartoon of 1786 shows Pitt handing a sack of money to George III and Queen Charlotte. To the right, a less-than-elegant Prince of Wales accepts a cheque from the French Duke of Orleans. Opponents accused Pitt of using Treasury funds to pay off royal debts.

Britain at sea

During the 18th century British naval power grew steadily. The three great voyages of exploration by Captain James Cook filled in vast blanks on the world map, and began Britain's association with Australia and New Zealand. In India, the East India Company, with its fleet of ships and army, ousted French competition. The British Empire was taking shape.

1783–1830: Reigns of George III, George IV and William IV

In 1783 William Pitt the Younger moved into Downing Street. Second son of Pitt the Elder and Lady Hester Grenville, and an MP for just two years, Pitt was at 24 Britain's youngest-ever Prime Minister (1783–1801, 1804–06), proving himself 'not a chip off the old block … but the block itself' according to Edmund Burke. Pitt had the ear of the king. In 1780 the Commons had passed a motion declaring that 'the influence of the Crown has increased, is increasing and ought to be diminished'. George III loathed liberals like Charles James Fox, who cheered the French Revolution of 1789. He trusted Pitt to fight social upheaval and France. Pitt brought in income tax; regularized East India Company rule with his 1784 India Act; and formalized Canada's dual British and French traditions. A friend of William Wilberforce, Pitt supported the anti-slavery movement, but did little to reform the voting system or settle the vexed 'Irish question'.

Henry Addington (1801–04) negotiated the Treaty of Amiens with France in 1802. Pitt returned (1804–06) to forge the Third Coalition alliance of Britain, Russia, Austria and Sweden; and after Nelson's victory at Trafalgar (1805) declared in a Guildhall speech: 'England has saved herself by her exertions, and will, as I trust, save Europe by her example.' A lonely, driven man, Pitt died exhausted in January 1806.

1740s–1830: Evolution and Revolution

LEFT: Captain James Cook's three epic voyages opened up vast new regions for British trade and colonization. This painting by William Hodges (1744–97) shows Cook and his men in the New Hebrides in 1774.

Lord Grenville (1806–07) led the Whig 'Ministry of All the Talents', but gave way to the Tory Duke of Portland (1807–09). The slave trade was abolished, but the dominant mood was cautious. Britain was still at war with Napoleon, and the old order trembling. Spencer Perceval (1809–12) had the melancholy distinction of being the only Prime Minister to be assassinated – shot in the lobby of the House of Commons by a failed merchant named John Bellingham. Lord Liverpool (1812–27) – prudent and modest, or 'the arch mediocrity' according to Benjamin Disraeli – led the government that celebrated victory at Waterloo in 1815.

In 1820 George III died, and the Prince Regent was crowned George IV in gaudy splendour. The Cato Street conspiracy planned to assassinate the entire Cabinet, but was thwarted by a 'mole'. London's only non-military lawmen were the Bow Street Runners (a small, quasi-criminal band in red waistcoats, dating from 1750); on a tip-off, they stormed the plotters' hideout, and five would-be assassins went to the gallows. Replacing Liverpool in 1827, George Canning died soon after taking office and Viscount Goderich lasted less than four months. Wellington (the last duke to be Prime Minister) led a Tory ministry from 1828 to 1830; then George IV died, the resulting election was won by the Whigs, and a new era began with the accession of William IV.

LEFT: King George III, painted by William Beechey (1753–1839). A man of admirable domestic habits, George was accused by radical critics of trying to increase royal power at the expense of Parliament. His severe bouts of mental illness complicated the tensions between the monarch and his ministers.

Duels

Politicians' clashes were occasionally more than merely verbal. Pitt duelled with fellow MP George Tierney in 1798, and in 1809 Foreign Secretary George Canning fought War Minister Lord Castlereagh. In 1829, the Duke of Wellington met the Earl of Winchelsea at Battersea to settle a dispute over what Wellington regarded as insulting remarks. Wellington fired his pistol first, apparently to miss (though it was suggested his opponent's lapel was torn). Winchelsea then fired in the air; an apology was accepted, and honour satisfied.

1830s–1880s: The Great Victorians

1830–1860s: Reigns of William IV and Queen Victoria

George IV died unlamented; ridiculed by satirists, a national embarrassment – his extravagance and amours had finally ceased to entertain. William IV, 'the sailor king' or 'Silly Billy', had been a Whig when his father George III was pro-Tory, but switched to Tory as soon as his own government was Whig. Wellington moved out, and Earl Grey (1830–34) came into Downing Street with a reformist agenda: the Reform Act of 1832, laws to restrict the employment of children in mines and factories, and the abolition of slavery in British territories. After Grey, Viscount Melbourne (1834) could not get on with the king and soon resigned; Wellington returned to hold five top posts himself for a month until Sir Robert Peel returned to London to take over (1834–35). Unable to form a majority, Peel gave way to Melbourne again (1835–41).

ABOVE: A lithograph by John Doyle shows Melbourne (1779–1848) riding with the newly crowned Queen Victoria in 1837. With them, evidently in his usual lively mood, is Palmerston (1784–1865), then Foreign Secretary.

In 1837, William IV died. His niece Victoria became queen, and her long reign (1837–1901) restored the monarchy's reputation. Melbourne acted as father figure to the young queen. She was less at ease with Peel, Prime Minister again from 1841 to 1846. The son of a Lancashire cotton manufacturer turned MP, the handsome Peel could seem aloof, but he was a superb administrator. As Home Secretary under Liverpool, he had set up London's first police force, the 'bobbies'. His 'Peelite' backers drew support from the middle classes, who thought the Prime Minister's repeal of the Corn Laws (1846) a liberal measure against the landed gentry. Peel also kept the lid on simmering radicalism, symbolized by the Chartist rallies of the 1840s. He resigned in 1846 (following a defeat on an Irish bill) but remained an MP; in 1850, the day after he'd spoken against Palmerston's foreign policy, Peel was thrown from his horse in Constitution Hill and died two days later.

The Whig Lord John Russell succeeded Peel as Prime Minister (1846–52). A Factory Act was passed (1847), there were attempts to reform the Poor Laws, and the Great Exhibition (1851) was a demonstration of national confidence. The Earl of Derby (1852) was followed by the Earl of Aberdeen, whose coalition government (1852–55) led the country into the Crimean War. Aberdeen – a keen archaeologist (he brought back a marble foot from the Parthenon) who had been present at the battle of Leipzig (1813) – wore mourning black for the rest of his life after the death of his wife in 1812. The war in the Crimea led to his downfall, and Aberdeen's replacement by Viscount Palmerston (1855–58 and 1859–65). Derby briefly again intervened in 1858–59.

ABOVE: Sir Robert Peel (1788–1850), a painting by William Essex, in the House of Commons. Peel was a pillar of the evolving Conservative party.

LEFT: The Houses of Parliament on fire, 16 October 1834, painting by an unknown artist. The rambling medieval Palace of Westminster was largely destroyed after a House of Lords furnace overheated and set off a massive blaze. Charles Barry's Gothic design, with interiors by A.W.N. Pugin, rose from the ashes.

Popular 'Pam' (as Palmerston was nicknamed) was energetic and bellicose, ever-ready to send in the Navy: he did so in 1850 while Foreign Secretary to pressurize Greece after David Pacifico, a British citizen in Athens, had his house burnt down. Any Briton could 'feel confident that the watchful eye and the strong arm of England will protect him against injustice and wrong'. Palmerston brought the Crimean War to an end, and had to manage the Indian Mutiny (1857–58) and a diplomatic fence-balancing act during the American Civil War. Notoriously unpunctual – 'the Palmerstons will always miss the soup', society hosts grumbled – Palmerston was a notorious chaser after housemaids, until settling down following a late marriage at 55 to Melbourne's sister. Still active into his 80s, he died in office in 1865.

Party politics

National party organizations were unknown in the mid 19th century. Few leaders gave public speeches, usually working within a close circle of intimates and colleagues, often relatives. Contested elections, with public voting rather than a secret ballot, were a rarity, and blatant voting 'irregularities' were regarded as normal practice.

Britain under steam

Britain got its first public steam railway in 1825 (Stockton to Darlington). In 1830, William Huskisson was the first MP to be killed by a train, knocked down at the opening of the Liverpool-Manchester line. By 1840, Britain had 4,000km (2,500 miles) of railways, linking London with the fast-growing industrial cities. Among the heroes of the age were engineers George and Robert Stephenson, and Isambard Kingdom Brunel.

Palmerston's successor was Lord John Russell. In his second term (to June 1866), Russell was opposed by his Cabinet when he tried to extend voting reform to the towns. Reform was brought in (1867) by Derby's third Conservative ministry (1866–68). After the Liberals (as the Whigs had now become) won a thumping election victory in 1868, Britain entered a notable parliamentary duel: the rivalry between Disraeli and Gladstone.

Gladstone and Disraeli

Both Disraeli and Gladstone began their prime ministerial careers in 1868. Disraeli got into Downing Street first.

London-born, of a Jewish family with Italian/Portuguese origins, Benjamin Disraeli was raised a Christian from the age of 13 – a decisive fact since Jews (by religion) were excluded from Parliament until 1858. He made his name as a youthful novelist, and acquired a dubious reputation for debt and love affairs, before becoming an MP in 1837 – his foppish dress and mannerisms attracting ridicule in the Commons. He married the widowed Mrs Wyndham Lewis in 1839; she later remarked, 'Dizzy married me for my money, but if he had the chance again he would marry me for love.' Disraeli's gift was vision; he saw the possibilities of empire abroad, culminating in the bestowal of the title Empress of India on the queen in 1876.

ABOVE RIGHT:
W. E. Gladstone (1809–98). He entered Parliament in 1832 (as a Tory) to become the most distinguished Liberal parliamentarian of his generation. His earnest manner though could appear tedious: Queen Victoria complained that Gladstone 'always addresses me as if I were a public meeting'.

RIGHT: 'Bowing him out', an 1880 caricature by 'GT' (J. Gordon Thomson); Disraeli, as king, is shown the door by his victorious successor, Gladstone.

Disraeli's first ministry lasted less than a year. Gladstone and the Liberals swept into power in December 1868. The two were now leaders of their evolving parties: Disraeli of the Conservatives/Tories; Gladstone of the Liberals/Whigs. Liverpool-born William Ewart Gladstone was of Scots stock. His path to the top began at Eton and Oxford – to 2010, Eton had produced 19 Prime Ministers. In a parliamentary career lasting more than 60 years, Gladstone became the 'Grand Old Man' of Liberalism; as Prime Minister (four times), his weakness probably lay in trying to do much himself. Never a favourite of Queen Victoria, who much preferred the wit of Disraeli, Gladstone was admired for his integrity; his habit of walking the streets to persuade prostitutes to abandon their calling might nowadays be misinterpreted, but to some Victorians this was the natural response of high-minded public duty to moral crisis.

Schools for all

Education was a main area for reform for 19th-century politicians. The endowed 'public' schools, like Eton, improved thanks to reformers such as Thomas Arnold of Rugby, and the success of the fictional *Tom Brown's Schooldays* by Thomas Hughes (1857). But there were no schools for many, until the 1870 Education Act provided cheap schooling for 5 to 11-year-olds; free primary schooling for all came in 1891.

1830s–1880s: The Great Victorians

The Liberal programme included Army and trade union reforms, changes in local and civil service administration, and an Education Act (1870). Disraeli returned in 1874, and persuaded Queen Victoria to re-enter public life after years of seclusion following the death of her consort, Prince Albert. Disraeli bought shares in the Suez Canal Company for Britain, and returned from the Congress of Berlin (1878) promising 'peace with honour' in Europe, while the great powers carved up Africa between them. Created Earl of Beaconsfield in 1876, Disraeli lost the 1880 election after damaging setbacks in Afghanistan and the Zulu War in South Africa; he retired to write his last novel and died in 1881, the queen laying a wreath on his coffin.

Gladstone soldiered on. His second ministry (1880–85) saw the first Boer War, the Married Women's Property Act, a new Reform Act (1884) and the failure to rescue General Gordon from Khartoum. When the Liberals lost the 1885 election, the Marquess of Salisbury (Robert Gascoyne-Cecil) led a brief Conservative government. Gladstone returned in 1886, but his party split over Ireland, and Salisbury held office until 1892 when Gladstone came back at the age of 82, still battling to pass Irish Home Rule. Defeated, he retired in 1894, and died four years later at his Cheshire home, Hawarden, where the 'Grand Old Man' of politics had long enjoyed his relaxation of tree-felling.

The Commons
Gladstone and Disraeli sparred in the still relatively new House of Commons, 1847, designed by Sir Charles Barry and A.W.N. Pugin. The old Palace of Westminster had burned down in 1834. The Victorian Commons chamber was itself destroyed by a German firebomb during the Blitz of 1941 and rebuilt 1945–50.

ABOVE: By the 1890s, most children received at least primary education. These pupils at Caverswall National School in Staffordshire do not look overjoyed at their improving situation.

The Primrose League
The Conservative enthusiasm for established Church, and imperial values, was embodied in the Primrose League. Founded in 1883 by Lord Randolph Churchill (father of Winston) and other leading Tories, its emblem was supposedly Disraeli's favourite flower.

ABOVE: Benjamin Disraeli (1804–81): heckled during his first Commons speech in 1837 for his over-elaborate language and showiness, he concluded 'though I sit down now, the time will come when you will hear me.' In 1872 he described the government front bench as 'a range of exhausted volcanoes', and in an 1878 banquet speech called Gladstone 'a sophistical rhetorician inebriated with the exuberance of his own verbosity'.

1890s–1922: Imperial Sunset

Salisbury Gives Way to the Liberals

Rosebery's brief Liberal administration (1894–95) ended when the Liberals split over expanding the Navy, and the Conservative Lord Salisbury returned to office in June 1895. Salisbury came from a famous family – his ancestors included Elizabeth I's counsellor, also named Robert Cecil. In Parliament since 1857, he for a time resorted to journalism, after a marriage which displeased his father; Disraeli commented that this experience made him 'a great master of jibes'. Salisbury had left the Commons in 1868 for the Lords, and succeeded Disraeli as Conservative leader. Combining the jobs of Prime Minister and Foreign Secretary much of the time, Salisbury presided over the high point of Victorian imperialism, symbolized by the royal Jubilees of 1887 and 1897. Salisbury (probably the tallest and the last bearded Prime Minister) left Downing Street in July 1902, having seen out the last years of Queen Victoria's reign, and the national disquiet over the Boer War in South Africa. He died in 1903.

ABOVE: Lord Salisbury (1830–1903) addressing the House of Lords. A lifelong student of science and theology, he seldom allowed emotion to influence his decisions or speeches. A firm believer in 'the spirit of the old constitution', he still warned fellow-Conservatives that 'the object of our party is not and ought not to be simply to keep things as they are'.

RIGHT: An illustration from the *Girls' Own Paper* (1900) of Grenadier Guards leaving Waterloo Station in London, on their way to the war in South Africa. The Boer War aroused patriotic fervour but also divided political opinion.

In 1901, the throne passed to Edward VII, the 'first gentleman of Europe'. The new Prime Minister from 1902 was Salisbury's nephew Arthur Balfour; their unique uncle/nephew partnership in British politics gave rise, it's said, to the expression 'Bob's your uncle'. Balfour, a millionaire at 21 through inheritance, was formidably intelligent, writing books on philosophy and socializing with academics. Edward VII could not take to him, even though both shared an enthusiasm for the Entente Cordiale alliance with France, to counter the threat from Germany. Balfour found his Cabinet fracturing, as Conservatives and Unionists argued over free trade within the empire; having lost support, he resigned in December 1905.

A changing world

Society was changing: cars on the roads, planes in the air, and new technology (telephones, radio, cinema) to marvel at. Britain's first purpose-built cinema opened in 1907, at Colne in Lancashire. Yet studies such as Seebohm Rowntree's (1901) showed almost 30 per cent of the population living in poverty.

ABOVE: The first 'hotline': Salisbury (left) uses a new telephone link between Britain and France to chat to France's President Carnot. This Tenniel drawing appeared in *Punch*, 28 March 1891.

ABOVE: Queen Victoria celebrated her Golden Jubilee in 1887. This book illustration was one of many regal images made to commemorate 50 years of her reign. Salisbury was Prime Minister for both this event and the Diamond Jubilee of 1897.

BELOW: Arthur Balfour (1848–1930) sets off for a drive. He succeeded his uncle, Lord Salisbury, as Prime Minister in July 1902, and served as Foreign Secretary during the First World War. He reportedly said that 'conservative prejudices are rooted in a great past and liberal ones planted in an imaginary future'.

The new Prime Minister was Henry Campbell-Bannerman – the first Prime Minister to be named in lists of official precedence, ranking fourth among the king's subjects after the archbishops of Canterbury and York and the Lord Chancellor. A man who, a house guest observed, would bow 'good morning' to his favourite trees, he was respected for his sincerity and good nature – 'the least cynical of mankind' according to Herbert Henry Asquith. Campbell-Bannerman won a convincing victory in the 1906 election, but died in 1908 and Asquith took over. The Lancastrian son of a nonconformist weaver, Asquith had won a scholarship to Oxford and become an MP in 1886. Home Secretary under Gladstone, but then in opposition for eleven years, he had pursued a legal career while out of office, unusual for the time.

Asquith was Prime Minister for almost nine years (1908–16), the longest term since Lord Liverpool. He brought in free school meals (1907), old age pensions (1908) and the 1911 Parliament Act ended the House of Lords' veto power over Commons' finance legislation. Pressing problems of the day included Irish Home Rule, still unresolved, and the campaign for votes for women. Edward VII died in 1910, and his son George V became king; but continuity was deceptive, for an era seemed to end in the summer of 1914 as Europe mobilized for 'the war to end all wars'.

The First World War

With European alliances and imperial support, and naval rearmament having delivered new battleships to the Royal Navy, national confidence was high in 1914. In May 1915, Asquith formed a coalition government, with Commons star David Lloyd George as minister of munitions. Asquith was not a war leader, his 'wait-and-see' policy hardly a recipe for victory. By 1916, with the failure of the Dardanelles expedition, the stalemate trench battles on the Western Front and the shock of the Easter Rising in Ireland, the country, led by the press, turned against Asquith. He resigned, and Lloyd George took his place, though Asquith remained leader of the Liberal party until 1926. Honoured with an earldom as the Earl of Oxford and Asquith (1925), he became a Garter knight shortly afterwards, but still turned to writing to supplement his income; he died in 1928.

ABOVE: H. H. Asquith (1852–1928); famous for the advice 'wait and see' (speeches during 1910). A Lancastrian, his legal career faltered after a brilliant academic start at Oxford University, and in 1886 he entered Parliament, where he flourished. Commentators observed that from the outset he spoke with the authority of a leader and not as a backbencher.

RIGHT: Emmeline Pankhurst (1858–1928), the suffragette leader, speaking in Trafalgar Square, London. The campaign for votes for women was long and often bitter, eventually succeeding after the First World War.

Votes for women

The decades-old campaign for votes for women came to a head with the activities of the Women's Social and Political Union. Led by Mrs Pankhurst, its direct action (which involved jail and hunger strikes) divided opinion; there was no women's suffrage legislation before the First World War. Women finally got the vote in 1918, after four years of war in which more than four million women worked on the home front.

1890s–1922: Imperial Sunset

Born in 1863 (while Palmerston was Prime Minister), David Lloyd George was brought up in Wales in a Liberal nonconformist tradition; Welsh was his first language. His eloquence, emotion and biblical fervour illuminated the Commons, but he had many enemies and his personal life was complicated: incapable of fidelity, he had a long, affair-strewn marriage before (in 1943), a second union to his secretary/lover Frances Stevenson. He and his friend Winston Churchill (who was at the Admiralty when the war began) were equally unpopular in some quarters: the hunting Duke of Beaufort commented that he would love to see 'Winston Churchill and Lloyd George in the middle of 20 couple of dog-hounds'.

ABOVE: David Lloyd George (1863–1945) inspects troops during the First World War.

Lloyd George narrowly escaped being drowned in 1916 when HMS *Hampshire* was sunk with Lord Kitchener en route to Russia: as munitions minister, he'd been an intended passenger. Balfour was for a time Foreign Secretary, his tenure remembered today for the 'Balfour Declaration' of November 1917 in favour of Zionist aspirations for a Jewish national state in Palestine. Lloyd George prosecuted the war with vigour, concentrating power in the hands of a small war cabinet. He talked to trade unions to ensure industrial efficiency, combated the German submarine threat, boosted farm production and brought in food rationing. He did not think highly of Britain's commanding generals on the Western Front, Haig and Robertson; at one stage in 1917 he offered to place the British Army under French command, to the generals' horror. When the Armistice came in November 1918, Lloyd George maintained wartime coalition politics, though Asquith declined to join. The 'Welsh Wizard' was one of the three top statesmen at the Versailles peace conference, along with Woodrow Wilson of the United States and Georges Clemenceau of France.

Post-war Britain faced an uncertain future, wounded by war and uncertain of its direction. No Prime Minister of any party was to find the 1920s and 1930s easy going.

ABOVE: One of several in a series of First World War posters showing Lord Kitchener urging volunteers to join the Army.

> **The war effort**
>
> Lloyd George had opposed the Boer War in South Africa, but in 1914 declared that the First World War was a fight for freedom on behalf of 'little nations' such as Belgium and Serbia. The War Cabinet was backed up by a Cabinet office and private secretaries, a Prime Ministerial style close to that of today. Volunteers flocked to join the Army but by May 1916 male conscription (for those aged 18 to 45) had been introduced, as Lloyd George vowed to 'fight to the finish.'

The 1920s and 1930s

ABOVE: James Ramsay MacDonald (1866–1937). After schooling that ended when he was 12, he worked as a pupil-teacher, clerk and journalist before entering Parliament in 1906. His opposition to the First World War cost him his Commons seat in 1918. Two years after his re-election in 1922, MacDonald found himself in Downing Street as Britain's first Labour Prime Minister.

Lloyd George was Prime Minister until 1922, promising 'a land fit for heroes' and to squeeze defeated Germany 'till the pips squeak'. With Conservative agreement, he opened negotiations with Irish nationalists, resulting in the treaty (1921) which divided Ireland. However, he faced accusations that peerages were being sold to buy support, and the coalition fractured. Asquith was still party leader, and Lloyd George found his support amongst the working class draining away in an atmosphere of post-war industrial disharmony. The Conservatives won an easy election victory.

The new Prime Minister was Andrew Bonar Law (1922–23). A Canadian, he was the first Prime Minister to be born outside the British Isles. He resigned because of ill health and died six months later. His Chancellor of the Exchequer, Stanley Baldwin, took over. The son of a Midlands industrialist, Baldwin was related to author and poet Rudyard Kipling and painter Sir Edward Burne-Jones. His government lasted barely six months, and in January 1924 in came James Ramsay MacDonald to lead Britain's first Labour government. MacDonald was an odd mixture: the Lossiemouth-born son of an unmarried housemaid, his Utopian visions of international harmony were at odds with the harsh economic reality; his Labour government collapsed in under a year, and Baldwin was back.

With Winston Churchill his Chancellor of the Exchequer, Baldwin survived the 1926 General Strike, but at the 1929 election his 'safety first' slogan failed to win enough votes. MacDonald returned as Prime Minister and appointed Britain's first female minister, Margaret Bondfield. The world crisis deepened with the 1929 Wall Street Crash, and

ABOVE: Chequers, the official country home of Britain's Prime Ministers since the 1920s. It provides security and seclusion away from London and the media. This painting was commissioned by the House of Commons in 2004.

The emergence of Labour

The 19th century saw the growth of working-class political power through electoral reform, the trade unions and the adoption of 'socialism' as an alternative to Liberalism. Keir Hardie founded the Independent Labour Party in 1893. The Labour Representation Committee (1900) was backed by the Fabian Society (1884) whose members included Beatrice and Sidney Webb, George Bernard Shaw and H.G. Wells. Two Labour MPs were elected in 1900. Labour ministers joined the wartime government in 1915, and Labour's strength had grown significantly by the 1920s.

ABOVE: In May 1926 Britain was in the grip of a General Strike. Here office workers watch a food convoy with military escort passing through the City of London.

Back from the wilderness

Winston Churchill, a Liberal after leaving the Conservatives in 1904, fought the 1922 general election from a wheelchair, while recovering from appendicitis. He lost. He wrote his book *The World Crisis* to pass the time and make some money, and bought his Kent country house Chartwell with the proceeds. Re-elected in 1924 as an independent, he was invited to rejoin the Conservatives by Stanley Baldwin, who made him Chancellor of the Exchequer.

few politicians had ready answers; MacDonald resigned in 1931 but was immediately reappointed leader of a national government, with Liberal and Conservative support. This 'betrayal' led to his expulsion from the Labour Party. In 1935, he switched jobs with Baldwin to become Lord President of the Council. He quit politics in May 1937, dying later that year on a ship bound for South America.

Baldwin tried to offer reassuring tranquillity, but his last years as Prime Minister (1935–37) saw clouds of war gathering. Government critics demanded rearmament to counter Fascism. At home, Baldwin eased the nation through the 1936 abdication crisis brought about by Edward VIII's desire to marry Mrs Simpson; he then resigned, took an earldom and retired. His successor was Chancellor of the Exchequer Neville Chamberlain who came from a distinguished Birmingham family; his father Joseph had been an imperial free-trader under Salisbury, and his brother Austen held several posts including Foreign Secretary under Baldwin in the 1920s. Neville Chamberlain's first flight in an aeroplane took him to Munich in 1938 for his fateful meeting with Adolf Hitler; he returned with the hope of peace, but was soon preparing Britain for war. He stayed Prime Minister through the first eight months of the Second World War, stepping down in May 1940. Already ailing, he died before the end of the year.

ABOVE: Stanley Baldwin (right; 1867–1947) outside Westminster Abbey with the Prince of Wales (later Edward VIII). In 1936, Edward's insistence on marrying Wallis Simpson (divorced and American) led to his abdication. Prime Minister Baldwin steered monarchy and country through the crisis in his customary low-key style.

Commonwealth and nationalism

During the 1920s and 1930s, imperial policy played a prominent part in British politics. Australia and Canada had moved to full dominion status, and there was much debate about the future of India. Closer to home, the foundation of Plaid Cymru (1925) and the Scottish National Party (1934) foreshadowed the devolution arguments of later decades.

LEFT: On 3 October 1938 Neville Chamberlain (1869–1940) waved a paper on which peace hopes briefly rested; the Prime Minister flew home from his Munich meeting with Hitler, believing that the Nazi dictator had put his signature to a binding appeasement agreement. In the Commons, Churchill called Munich 'a total unmitigated defeat'.

1940–1955: War and Peace

When the Second World War began on 3 September 1939, Winston Churchill returned to the Admiralty (which he had first entered as Navy minister in 1911). In the 1930s he had been labelled a warmonger for demanding rearmament; now he was the man in waiting when in May 1940 Chamberlain resigned. The new Prime Minister took personal charge of the war effort, heading an all-party government and the War Cabinet, which included Labour leader Clement Attlee.

Churchill was tireless: cajoling, scheming, exhorting and interfering, and offering opinions on everything from amphibious landings to air-raid shelters, passing many nights in the subterranean Cabinet War Rooms in London during the Blitz. He pinned his hopes for victory on the United States, which entered the war in December 1941, and Churchill's friendship with US President Roosevelt became central to Allied strategy. In 1943 Churchill, Roosevelt and the Soviet leader Stalin met at Tehran (Iran) to agree plans for the D-Day landings in June 1944 which marked the beginning of the end of the war in Western Europe; Churchill wanted to go with the invasion troops, but was told by George VI to stay at home. In May 1945 crowds in London celebrated VE-Day, and Churchill joined the Royal Family on the balcony of Buckingham Palace. Within a month he had left Downing Street. At the general election held in June 1945, Labour won a massive victory and Clement Attlee became Prime Minister.

ABOVE RIGHT: 11 September 1940, Churchill with King George VI and Queen Elizabeth inspect bomb damage at Buckingham Palace after an enemy air raid.

RIGHT: The 'Big Three' Allied leaders – Churchill, Roosevelt and Stalin – met at Yalta in the Crimea, in February 1945. Churchill was discussing post-war reorganization but within six months he was no longer Prime Minister.

In 20 years as Labour leader (1935–55), Attlee exuded calm, pipe-smoking imperturbability. A Liberal lawyer's son, he started off as a Conservative but became a socialist after seeing for himself the poverty in East London. During the First World War he was an infantry major and badly wounded. Attlee was MP for Limehouse from 1922 to 1950, and thereafter for Walthamstow West. He succeeded George Lansbury as party leader in 1935, and from 1940 served in the War Cabinet as Lord Privy Seal, then deputy Prime Minister (from 1942). As Prime Minister Attlee presided over historic changes: independence and partition in India, the birth of the United Nations, the Berlin Airlift and the Cold War, and at home the creation of the National Health Service, the modern welfare state, and nationalisation of Britain's coal mines and railways. He held together a Cabinet of diverse personalities and opinions, as Britain struggled to rebuild after six years at war and find a new role in a world dominated by two super-powers: the United States and the Soviet Union.

LEFT: Clement Attlee (1883–1967) led Britain into an uncertain post-war world as Prime Minister of the Labour government in 1945. Here he confers with Foreign Secretary Ernest Bevin (left) at a UN meeting in London early in 1946; Britain was exhausted after six years of war, and the Cold War temperature was already dropping.

ABOVE: Churchill's bedroom in the London Churchill War Rooms. Sealed off from the bombing above, Prime Minister and staff worked in a somewhat claustrophobic warren beneath Whitehall to plot survival and victory in the Second World War.

Stirring stuff

Churchill's wartime speeches became legendary. On 13 May 1940 he told the House of Commons that Britain would fight 'with all the strength that God can give us'. He told the British people in a radio broadcast: 'we shall fight on the beaches, we shall fight on the landing grounds, we shall fight in the fields and in the streets, we shall fight in the hills; we shall never surrender.'

1940–1955: War and Peace

In 1951, the Conservatives won a narrow election victory, and Churchill returned as Prime Minister at the age of 76. Attlee remained Labour leader until 1955, thereafter taking an earldom. Churchill's last years as Prime Minister were dominated by the Korean War and international tensions between East and West. In 1952 King George VI died, and Churchill delighted in the pomp and ceremony of the coronation of the young Queen Elizabeth II in 1953; he was appointed a Knight of the Garter and also awarded the Nobel Prize for literature. Slowed by a stroke just before his 80th birthday, he resigned in April 1955, handing over to his Foreign Secretary and wartime colleague Sir Anthony Eden. Churchill remained an MP until 1964.

Eden had followed a traditional route for Prime Ministers – Eton and Christ Church, Oxford. He won the Military Cross in 1917, and was MP for Warwick and Leamington from 1923 until 1957. Foreign Secretary from 1935 to 1938, he had resigned in protest over the Munich deal, but held the post again in 1940–45 and 1951–55. Of great charm, Eden's best years were behind him when he entered Downing Street, and he was brought down by the ill-judged Suez operation in 1956, when he sent British forces to attack Egypt after President Nasser moved to take control of the Suez Canal. The Anglo-French operation ended in humiliating withdrawal after international pressure led by the United States. Eden resigned in January 1957 on the grounds of ill health.

> **Churchill's farewell**
>
> In 1963 Winston Churchill, whose mother, Jennie (Lady Randolph Churchill), was an American, was made an honorary citizen of the United States. President John F. Kennedy called him 'the most honored and honorable man to walk the stage of history in the time in which we live'. Churchill died on 24 January 1965 (the same date as his father, Lord Randolph Churchill, 70 years before), and was buried at Bladon in Oxfordshire, near his birthplace, Blenheim Palace.

LEFT: A hospital nurse in 1948, when the Attlee government launched Britain's National Health Service. Commonwealth immigrants were arriving to help as Britain struggled to rebuild a war-ravaged and ageing infrastructure.

ABOVE: The 27-year-old Queen Elizabeth II at her coronation in Westminster Abbey, 2 June 1953. 'New Elizabethan' hopes were mostly short-lived.

ABOVE: Sir Anthony Eden (1897–1977) at the microphone during the Suez crisis of 1956, which ended his prime ministerial career. The British and French occupation of the Suez Canal Zone, ahead of the invading Israeli army, was condemned by the United Nations and caused huge controversy in Britain. Eden resigned in January 1957.

1957–1979: Years of Uncertainty

Eden's dejected departure marked a watershed. Britain was no longer a world power; the Empire was evolving into the Commonwealth of independent nations and British politicians cast about for a new role.

Eden's successor as Prime Minister was Harold Macmillan (1957–63). Grandson of one of two Scots brothers who founded the Macmillan publishing firm in the 19th century, Macmillan had been wounded during the First World War, and (like Eden) was awarded a Military Cross. A critic of appeasement in the 1930s, he had served as a junior member in the wartime government, and in the early 1950s had been in charge of housing. After spells as Chancellor of the Exchequer and Foreign Secretary under Eden, he beat R.A. Butler to the top job.

Behind his tweedy grouse-moor image, a gift to cartoonists, Macmillan was a shrewd operator and a modernizer, at ease on radio and television. At home he offered material improvement ('you've never had it so good …'), while abroad he played the wise elder statesman at summit meetings with Eisenhower and Kennedy, and Soviet leader Khrushchev. In 1960 he spoke of a 'wind of change' blowing through Africa. Pro-European, he began talks about UK membership of the European Community; but these foundered on the rock of General de Gaulle's opposition. The 1963 Profumo affair and the Philby spy scandal shook Macmillan's government, and illness finally brought his resignation. To the surprise of most commentators, Tory grandees chose a peer, the Earl of Home, to succeed 'Supermac'. The Earl won election to the Commons, and as Sir Alec Douglas-Home was Prime Minister until the 1964 election, which ended 13 years of Tory rule and sent Labour back into power, with Harold Wilson.

ABOVE: Harold Macmillan (1894–1986) speaking at a Conservative fete in Bromley, Kent, in 1963, his final year in power.

Prime ministerial observations

Harold Wilson observed that 'the main essentials of a Prime Minister are sleep and a sense of history'. Harold Macmillan liked the job, commenting laconically: 'Interesting work. Fine town house. Nice place in the country. Servants. Plenty of foreign travel.'

RIGHT: Harold Wilson (1916–95) basks in the limelight with the Beatles in 1964. Wilson saw his reform agenda sag as Britain's economy nose-dived in the 1960s and 1970s. An adroit politician, he was particularly good at media sound-bites, such as 'A week is a long time in politics'. His pipe-smoking and favourite raincoat were perhaps not quite in tune with the 'Swinging 60s'.

Wilson projected himself as a populist and modernizer. Born in 1916 in Huddersfield, he was a former Oxford don who had entered Parliament in 1945, and succeeded Hugh Gaitskell as Labour leader in 1963. With a slender majority, Labour promised change and reform: it offered a National Plan and several new government departments (including Arts, Overseas Development and Sport). The 1966 election increased Labour's majority. Wilson had always seemed comfortable with the media, happy to appear alongside the Beatles and celebrate England's 1966 World Cup win, but his cheeriness faded as the economy sickened, and the pound was devalued. Not even the prospect of North Sea oil could save Labour from defeat in 1970, and Edward Heath formed a new Conservative administration.

ABOVE: Londonderry, 1969. Onlookers watch as a fire burns following a petrol bombing as the Northern Ireland troubles worsened.

LEFT: Edward Heath (1916–2005), the most Europhile of British prime ministers, signed the treaty of UK accession to the European Economic Community in 1973. On his right sat Sir Alec Douglas-Home (1903–95), former Prime Minister, back in his old job as Foreign Secretary.

Heath was an ardent Europhile and signed Britain into the European Community after overcoming French objections in 1972. He was less successful at home in an era of sharply rising energy prices, power cuts, strikes and the three-day week. Born in Broadstairs, Kent, and from a modest background, Heath was a bachelor, whose hobbies included music, conducting and yachting. His rather forced jocularity was much liked by impressionists. In 1974 Heath decided to test the issue of 'who governs' in an election: he lost, and Wilson was back in Number 10, with a minority government – Labour managed to boost their majority to three after a second election later that year.

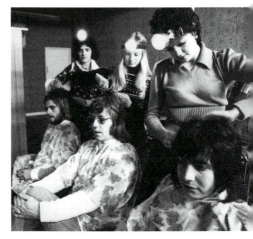

ABOVE: In 1974 an energy crisis resulted in most UK businesses being rationed to electricity for only three days a week. At this hairdressing salon in Chatham in Kent, staff wore battery-powered lamps as they trimmed the stylishly long 70s locks of its customers. Heath paid the price for such gloomy days.

All change

On 15 February 1971, Britons said farewell to pounds, shillings and pence. Instead, shoppers grappled with decimal coinage. Much-loved threepenny bits and half-crowns disappeared. The shilling became the 5p piece, the florin (two shillings) became 10p; and shopkeepers were widely blamed for taking advantage of the change to increase prices.

1957–1979: Years of Uncertainty

> ### Comings and goings
> James Callaghan's brief premiership saw some notable events: the deaths of Chairman Mao (1976) and Elvis Presley (1977); the first test-tube baby (1978); the Iranian revolution (1979) which deposed the Shah; and on British television, the last appearance of Dixon of Dock Green, and the arrival of Basil Fawlty.

ABOVE: James Callaghan pictured in 1979, his last year as Prime Minister.

BELOW: Anglo-French cooperation saw the arrival of Concorde in 1969; it came into service in 1976, with Callaghan, and was retired in 2003, under Blair.

The economy still struggled, but Wilson's abrupt resignation in 1976 came as a surprise. He seemed to have run out of energy, and there were suggestions that he had become convinced the security services were plotting to remove him. His successor was the usually unflappable 'sunny Jim' Callaghan. James Callaghan, born in Portsmouth in 1912, had risen from modest beginnings – he had been a tax officer, then served in the Royal Navy during the war. Another MP who entered the Commons in 1945, he had been both Chancellor and Foreign Secretary. Callaghan's term as Prime Minister was beset by economic woes and industrial unrest, culminating in the 'winter of discontent' (1978–79); he lost a vote of no-confidence in May 1979, and Labour crashed to defeat at the May 1979 election. Margaret Thatcher swept into Downing Street – the first woman to lead the Conservative Party (1975) and so far the only female Prime Minister in Britain's history.

> ### Prime ministerial records
> James Callaghan was the longest-lived British Prime Minister. He died in 2005 aged 92 years 364 days, just beating Harold Macmillan, who was 92 years 322 days old when he died in 1986. The oldest Prime Minister when first appointed was Palmerston, at 71. Gladstone was a veteran of 82 when he formed his last government.

1979–Present: Modern Britain

The Thatcher/Major Years

Few Prime Ministers divided opinions more sharply than Mrs Thatcher. Admired and disliked in equal measure, her place in history was assured as she left 10 Downing Street in 1990, after almost 12 years in office. A grocer's daughter, Margaret Hilda Roberts was born in Grantham in 1925, tasted student politics at Oxford University and worked as a research chemist; after her marriage to Denis Thatcher she studied law and first stood for Parliament in 1950. Elected Conservative MP for Finchley in 1959, she was given charge of education and science by Edward Heath, and to most people's surprise won the ballot to replace him as Conservative party leader in 1975. A decisive election win in 1979 brought her to power and she won two more elections (1983, 1987).

Thatcher had strong views, for example about 'wets' and 'drys' in her own party, and she divided opinions in the country. Her main aim was to limit state 'interference': to cut trade union power and public expenditure, privatize state-run enterprises (such as gas and electricity), maintain as much independence from European directives as possible, and run a tough monetary policy. Her decision to go to war with Argentina over the Falklands in 1982 was generally popular; she won a landslide victory in the 1983 election. But Thatcherism's 'surgery' left scars: unemployment soared to over three million; the coal miners' strike of 1984–85 was a bitter episode; and the proposed community charge, labelled a 'poll tax', led to riots. Northern Ireland's troubles spread violence to the mainland: two government ministers, Airey Neave and Ian Gow, were murdered by the IRA; so was Lord Mountbatten, and in 1984 Thatcher survived an IRA bomb attack on the Grand Hotel, Brighton, aimed at killing Cabinet members.

ABOVE: In April 1982, a Royal Navy task force set sail for the Falklands. Vowing to restore British sovereignty in the islands by ousting Argentine invasion troops, Mrs Thatcher declared in regal Victorian tones: 'Failure? The possibility does not exist.' The Falklands campaign was won by 14 June.

BELOW: Margaret Thatcher struck up a good relationship with US President Ronald Reagan, here visiting Downing Street in 1988 – the year after Thatcher's third consecutive general election victory.

Thatcher's decade

The 1980s saw the election of Ronald Reagan in 1980, and Britain's last African colony, Rhodesia, becoming Zimbabwe. This was the decade of the marriage of Prince Charles and Lady Diana Spencer in 1981; the Falklands task force in 1982; the anguish and violence of the miners' strikes of 1984–85; the Great Storm which tore down trees across southern England in 1987; and the Lockerbie bombing over Scotland in 1988.

As the 'Iron Lady', Margaret Thatcher exerted a powerful influence over her Cabinet, and she marched onto the world stage with vigour. She tussled with the European

> **Long terms**
>
> Mrs Thatcher was in Downing Street for almost 12 years. Ahead of her in terms of years (though only Liverpool and Walpole had unbroken spells in office) stand Gladstone (12 years), Salisbury (13), Liverpool (14), Pitt the Younger (18) and Walpole (20).

Community for rebates on British payments. She struck up a close relationship with US President Ronald Reagan and Soviet leader Mikhail Gorbachev, as the ice sheets of the Cold War melted, and Communism in Russia and eastern Europe started to crumble. But as a new decade dawned, the Conservatives split; Thatcher put her leadership to the test, and found her support withering. She resigned, shell-shocked, and was succeeded by John Major.

Major was a surprise choice, unostentatious and mild-mannered, the least flamboyant of top Tories. Born in 1943 in London, he was the son of a trapeze artiste, left school at 16 and worked in banking before entering the Commons in 1979. Mrs Thatcher promoted him swiftly, and he had just been made Chancellor of the Exchequer when he won the top job in November 1990. Major was Prime Minister during the first Gulf War (1991) and won re-election in 1992; he began moves towards peace in Northern Ireland, but opposition to Europe from the 'Maastricht rebels' within his own party weakened his position. Another blow came on 'Black Wednesday' (16 September 1992) when Britain was forced out of the European exchange rate mechanism. With Labour remodelled under first John Smith then Tony Blair, the political balance shifted; the 1997 election saw the Conservatives routed. John Major left Downing Street, and in came Tony Blair and New Labour.

ABOVE: Few industrial disputes in modern times caused more bitterness than the miners' strike of 1984. There were orderly protests, like this rally by Welsh mining families, but also violent battles between police and miners. The strike failed to prevent a nationwide pit-closure programme.

RIGHT: John Major, in typical relaxed style, meets Irish Prime Minister Albert Reynolds in Brazil in 1992. Improved relations between Britain and the Irish Republic helped in kick-starting moves towards a resolution of the troubles in Northern Ireland.

The Nineties and Noughties

Tony Blair was born in Edinburgh in 1953 – the first Prime Minister to be born after the Second World War. After Oxford University, he became a lawyer and was elected MP for Sedgefield in 1983. When Labour leader John Smith died suddenly in 1994, Blair was elected to succeed him, having made his mark as a Commons debater and a smooth media performer. As leader, he sought to widen 'New Labour' appeal by moving the party away from its traditional working class/trade union/leftist affiliations, and appealing to 'middle-ground' voters and business.

With more women MPs than ever before, women were prominent in Blair's Cabinet, though the Cabinet now played a less central role in government than an inner circle of advisers and 'spin doctors'. The key figure in the government was Chancellor of the Exchequer Gordon Brown, a close friend of Blair during Labour's years in opposition. An important change was to give independence to the Bank of England (which fixes interest rates). The Belfast agreement established a peace process in Northern Ireland; Hong Kong was returned to China; and devolution arrangements were agreed for Scotland and Wales.

Children in Number 10

Tony Blair was the first Prime Minister to become a father while in Number 10. He and his wife Cherie, a successful lawyer, had son Leo in May 2000, their fourth child. The Prime Minister with the largest family was reputedly Earl Grey in the early 19th century, whose children numbered 15.

ABOVE RIGHT: Tony Blair outside Number 10 with his family in June 2001. Labour had just won its second landslide election under Blair's leadership. With the Prime Minister (left to right): Nicholas, Kathryn, baby Leo, wife Cherie, and Euan.

RIGHT: The New Labour Cabinet, May 1997. Prime Minister Blair is flanked by Cabinet Secretary Sir Robin Butler, and John Prescott. Donald Dewar (third from left) became Scotland's First Minister in 1999 after devolution.